Shivers and Goose Bumps
How We Keep Warm

By Franklyn M. Branley

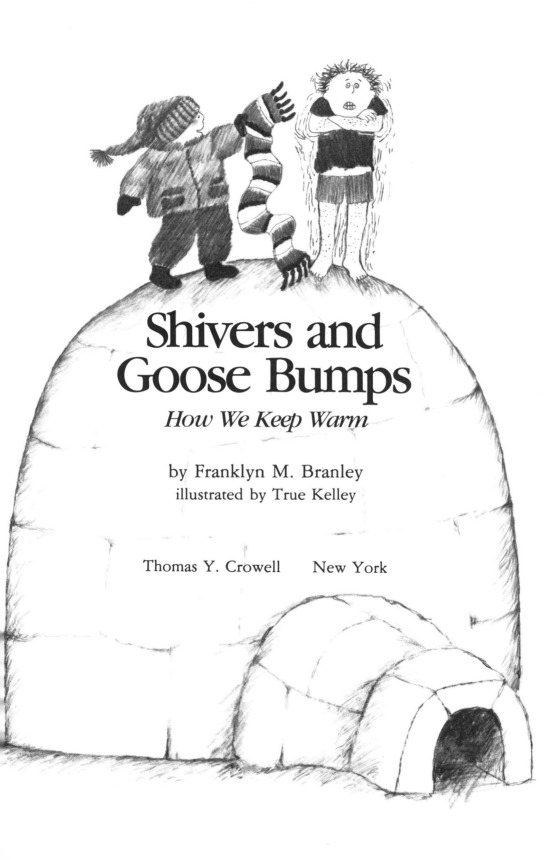

Shivers and Goose Bumps

How We Keep Warm

by Franklyn M. Branley
illustrated by True Kelley

Thomas Y. Crowell   New York

Library of Congress Cataloging in Publication Data
Branley, Franklyn Mansfield, 1915–
   Shivers and goose bumps.

   Summary: Describes how certain animals keep warm,
how the human body loses and retains its heat, and
how various types of clothing and dwellings aid in
heat retention.
   1. Body temperature—Regulation—Juvenile literature.
[1. Body temperature]   I. Kelley, True, ill.   II. Title.
QP135.B67 1984   599 ʹ.0188   82-45921
ISBN 0-690-04334-1
ISBN 0-690-04335-X (lib. bdg.)

2 3 4 5 6 7 8 9 10
First Edition

Contents

1. How Cold Can You Get?   6
   Shivers and Goose Bumps   10
2. Loss of Heat   14
   Radiation   16
   Convection   19
   Conduction   21
3. Eskimos Keep Warm—
   Desert Dwellers Keep Cool   24
   Shelters   29
   Igloos   32
   Cold-Weather Clothing   36
4. Birds in Winter   42
5. Black Bears in Winter   48
6. Heating Our Houses   52
   Solar and Electric Houses   64
7. Clothes Keep Us Warm   68
   Hypothermia   71
8. Keeping Warm in Outer Space   76
   High-Level Radiation   82
   Further Reading   89
   Index   91

1/How Cold Can

You Get?

Your body is a remarkable heat engine. You have a thermostat that "turns up the heat" when you're too cold, or cools you down when you get too warm.

Your temperature controls keep you at a steady "good health" temperature of 98.6° Fahrenheit. (Throughout this book we'll be using Fahrenheit temperatures. Should you wish to change them to Celsius, subtract 32 from the readings; then take ⅝ of the difference. For example; $98.6 - 32 = 66.6$, and ⅝ of 66.6 equals 37°C.) Temperatures usually vary a bit from 98.6°. The range is between 98.4° and 98.8°, although many people's good-health temperature is a degree or so lower. It would be interesting to take the temperatures of people in your class to see how much variation there is. When you exercise, your temperature may jump to 102° because all your body activities are speeded up.

Regardless of where you live, in the tropics or in the arctic regions, your body temperature remains close to what is normal for you. However, in very hot regions people must wear protective clothing to ward off the heat. And where it is very cold, the proper kind of warm clothing is essential, for without it a person could freeze to death.

As body temperatures drop, people shiver and stumble, the skin becomes blue and puffy. Below 80° they usually become unconscious, their reflexes fail to function, their hearts and breathing may fail, which means they will die.

But there are exceptions. The survival of Jean Hilliard of Fosston, a small town in northwest Minnesota, continues to puzzle doctors. Late in the night of December 19, 1980, Jean was returning home after visiting friends some ten miles away. But she never got there. During her visit a storm had blown in. Winds reached fifty miles an hour, and the temperature had dropped to 25° below zero.

She had her father's new car and was warm inside as she traveled the lonely back road. Without warning the car struck a patch of ice and slid sideways into a ditch. Jean tried to grind her way out but could not budge the car. There was only one thing to do: get out and walk to Wally Nelson's house, just down the road. He'd get his truck and pull out the car.

Jean was wearing only her jeans, for when she had started from home hours earlier, the temperature had been a lot higher. She bundled up in her light jacket and started walking. After a while she knew she was going in the wrong direction, so she retraced her steps. Every second she was getting colder. Her legs were like ice. After forty-five minutes she saw the lights of Wally's house. From then on her memory is blank.

Somehow she stumbled and staggered, slipped and crawled, from the hill to Wally's house. She reached his front porch. One more effort and she would have banged on the door. But that was impossible. She collapsed face-down and lay there for five hours in the snow and freezing cold.

The next morning at seven Wally set out for his job. He tried to open the door but it would go only halfway. Jean was blocking it. He looked at her gray, swollen face, and her motionless eyes that were frozen open. Wally thought she was dead, but then he heard a moan and knew she was still alive. She had to be taken as fast as possible to the emergency room of the hospital. Jean was frozen stiff; no part of her body would bend, so Wally had to place her crossways and at an angle in the back of the car.

At the hospital her body was black from the waist down. They could not put a needle into her, the skin was so hard. And she could not swallow—her throat muscles were frozen. She was so cold, her body temperature did not show up on a thermometer. Doctors figure that her temperature had dropped to 64°. The doctors shone a light into her eyes, but there was no movement. The first sign of life was a weak quiver of her heart. The spasms, which could not be called heartbeats, occurred only ten times a minute.

Jean was packed in heating pads filled with water. For hours warm water was pumped through the pads. Remarkably, Jean became conscious later that afternoon. The veins deep inside her body had not frozen. Slowly her temperature rose to normal.

But what would happen to her? She might have become brain damaged. Or, at best, her legs would probably have to be amputated. Miraculously, neither happened. After seven weeks of intense care Jean left the hospital. Her legs were still hard and dark, but slowly they too came to life. Years later she has recovered completely. Not even a toe had to be removed.

Doctors are at a loss to explain Jean's survival. Most people would have died, for hypothermia (death by freezing) usually occurs when body temperature drops to 78°.

We can't explain how she recovered either. But we do know that the body has many ways of adjusting to cold temperatures, and to high ones.

Shivers and Goose Bumps

When you're swimming, you may shiver as you come out of the water. That's especially true if there's a breeze. You wrap up in a towel to keep warm. But still you shiver, and your teeth chatter. Water is evaporating from your body, and the evaporation takes away heat.

You shiver because the muscles of your body are trying to produce heat to replace the heat you're losing. Most body heat is made in the muscles. In the cells oxygen is combined with carbohydrates and fats, producing energy. Animal bodies—including humans—"burn" food just as wood is burned in a fire, except that the process is slower in the body and so the heat is released gradually. Muscles always produce energy, sometimes more, sometimes less.

When you exercise, they are more active and so produce more heat. When you're losing heat rapidly, the best thing to do is jog around. If you don't, you'll shiver. That's the alternate way the muscles produce heat: They twitch. Another way of saying this is the muscles tighten and loosen rapidly; they vibrate. Next time you shiver, try running a bit. You'll find that after two or three minutes the shivering will stop. It's because running made your muscles produce more heat, so shivering was no longer needed to maintain body temperature.

One way bodies adjust to cold is by increasing heat production. Another way is by slowing down the loss of heat. That's what you're trying to do when you get goose bumps.

Birds and certain animals get much bigger goose bumps than we do. You can't see the bumps through their feathers or fur, but you can see their effects. If you've watched birds on a cold day, perhaps you've noticed how they fluff their feathers. They perch on branches and vibrate their feathers so much, they appear to become almost double their normal size.

What they're doing is making small spaces between their feathers. Dead air—so called because it does not move and circulate—becomes trapped in those spaces. And one of the best insulators (preventers of heat loss) is dead air. The more spaces there are, the more air becomes trapped; and the more dead air there is, the more heat is saved. The fluffed-up feathers become an insulating container preserving the bird's body heat. If you could see the bird's body, you would see that it is covered with goose bumps— a bump at every place where a feather is attached.

Animals with thick hair and fur do the same thing. Watch a cat, a dog, or a horse. On cold days they bristle their hair, fluff it up. The animal appears larger. That's because fluffing has surrounded the animal's body with a layer of trapped air. Once more, if you could see the animal's skin, you would see it covered with goose bumps—a bump for every hair.

Just as animals get goose bumps when they're cold, so do you. Everywhere a hair is attached, there's a goose bump. (You don't get them on your head because there are insufficient muscles in the scalp.) Your body is reacting in a primitive way to heat loss. At some time long past, it seems, your early ancestors had heavy hair over most of their bodies. In order to prevent heat loss, those early ancestors would have bristled their hair. And you still do. You get goose bumps. But the action isn't very effective in saving body heat, because you no longer have heavy hair on your body. Now you save body heat by using various kinds of clothing, which we'll talk about later.

Ordinarily the human body reacts to cold in a completely satisfactory manner. It generates more heat, and it also conserves heat. But it can be exposed to severe conditions where the outside temperature is so cold the body cannot maintain a normal temperature. Should you lose so much heat that your body temperature drops to between 91° and 95°, you would become unable to remember and unable to speak clearly. Should your temperature go lower, your muscles would become rigid, you would be unable to walk without stumbling, and your skin would turn blue and puffy. Below 78° the effects are usually fatal. Yet we know death doesn't always follow: Jean Hilliard survived a temperature that appears to have been no more than 64°.

2/Loss of Heat

You could say that "heat is something, while cold is nothing." And you would be about right. Cold is merely the absence of heat. The only way you can make anything cold is by taking heat away from it. When you put an ice cube in water, the water gets cold because as ice melts it takes heat away from the water. A refrigerator takes heat out of the box and puts the heat into the kitchen. You can feel the heat given off when your refrigerator is running.

You can feel heat transfer by wetting your hands and holding them in the air. The water evaporates, changing to water vapor. The heat required for this to occur comes from your hands, and so your hands feel cool. Water is always evaporating from your hands even when they feel dry. If you cover a hand with a plastic bag, it soon feels hot and clammy because evaporation cannot occur. Your body produces more heat than is needed to maintain normal temperature. A large part of the excess heat is lost by evaporation through pores in the skin. When you cannot get rid of that heat, you feel uncomfortable.

Evaporation can be speeded by removing your clothes. You'd be comfortable down to about 75°, but would get shivery as soon as the temperature dropped any lower. And evaporation can be speeded by moving the air that surrounds you. A fan makes you feel cooler; so does a natural breeze. Evaporation causes cooling, and the faster it occurs, the greater the cooling.

When you have a fever, meaning your body temperature is higher than 98.6°, you sometimes need to have an alcohol bath. Alcohol evaporates very rapidly—much faster than water—and the rapid evaporation often is sufficient to bring down the temperature of a feverish person.

In addition to losing heat by evaporation, your body loses heat in the breathing process. Air in your lungs is heated to body temperature. As the air is exhaled, whatever heat it has picked up is carried away.

Evaporation and breathing remove heat from your body. There are three principal ways in which the heat moves

away from you, and also moves toward you. The first is by radiation.

Radiation

When you turn on a lamp, light goes out from it in all directions. It radiates, and you are aware it's happening

because you can see it. At the same time, however, heat is radiating from the lamp. You may be able to feel it, but more often you cannot because there's not enough heat.

Anything that is warm radiates heat to everything that is cooler. For example, heat radiates from a hot stove or from a fireplace. And it radiates from you.

When you are in a room, most often you are warmer than the walls, chairs, tables, and other objects in the room. Therefore, heat radiates from you to those objects. Should there be a large temperature difference, radiation is more rapid. You would radiate heat very rapidly—lose it—and so become uncomfortable.

A large part of the heat you lose escapes by radiation. When you're asleep and covered by little more than a sheet, 53% of your heat loss is by radiation. Another 28% is by evaporation, and the remaining 19% by convection, processes that are discussed later.

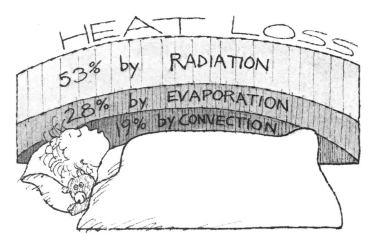

RADIANT HEAT

Some houses are heated by radiation and are very comfortable. Electric wires or hot-water pipes may be imbedded in the walls, ceilings, or floors, so that large surfaces of the room are warmed. The walls, ceilings, and floors do not pick up radiation rapidly from people's bodies. Heat is not lost so quickly, and so people feel more comfortable.

You can slow down cooling by radiation by wearing the proper clothing. Clothes tend to reflect heat back to the body, much as light is reflected from mirrors. Unfortunately, the effect is greatest when the reflecting surface is smooth, just as reflection of light from a mirror is greatest when the mirror is smooth. Most clothing therefore does not reduce radiation loss very much. In order to do so, the clothing would have to be lined with a smooth reflector of some sort. And that might make it rather awkward to move about.

However, certain types of thermal blankets are quite effective in decreasing radiation loss when you're in bed. The blankets are made of layers of plastic and metal foil, or foil-coated plastic. The plastic slows down evaporation (it works the way the plastic bag does when you put your hand into it), and the foil reflects radiant heat. It can do this because a blanket is spread out more or less smoothly, so the foil remains much flatter than it would if the foil were used in clothing.

Convection

Heat moves from place to place by radiation; it goes up, down, sideways—in all directions. Also, it moves best when no air is present. For example, heat loss by radiation occurs very rapidly in outer space.

When air or water is present, heat may be lost by radiation. But it is also lost, or moved from place to place, by convection—by movements of the air or water. Warmer gas or liquid tends to move upward so it "floats" atop colder masses. As the heated material rises, the colder descends to take its place and a movement called a convection current is set up.

You cannot readily see convection currents in air, but there's an easy way to see them in a liquid.

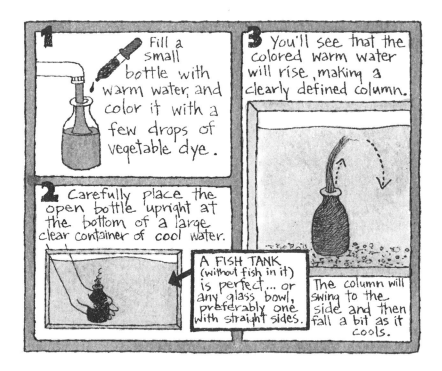

1. Fill a small bottle with warm water, and color it with a few drops of vegetable dye.

2. Carefully place the open bottle upright at the bottom of a large clear container of cool water.

A FISH TANK (without fish in it) is perfect... or any glass bowl, preferably one with straight sides.

3. You'll see that the colored warm water will rise, making a clearly defined column.

The column will swing to the side and then fall a bit as it cools.

Try reversing temperatures to see what happens, if anything. Put warm water in the larger container, and cold colored water in the smaller bottle. You'll find that in order for convection to occur, the lower temperature must be placed above the higher temperature.

In houses, radiators are placed beneath windows. Air around the radiators is heated, and it therefore rises past the windows. The warmed air goes toward the ceiling, where it is deflected toward the inner part of the room. As the air moves, it cools somewhat and so descends along the inside wall of the room. A convection current moves through the room. (At the same time heat is also radiating from the radiator to all cooler objects in the room.)

Your body also sets up convection currents, because your temperature is greater than the temperature of the

CONVECTION CURRENTS

warm air
cool air
ceiling
inner wall
radiator
warm body
cool air near floor

air in the room. The air immediately around you becomes heated. This air moves upward, and it tends to float on the cooler air that is near the floor. (In a cold room, your feet become coldest first because the cold air tends to "hug" the floor.) Your body heat sets up a small convection current that carries heat away from you. You become a sort of chimney, so warm air moves up and away from you.

In order for convection currents to start, the air around you must become heated. In part, this is done by conduction.

Conduction

The convection current discussed above occurs because the air around you is heated by contact. The air touches you and heat is conducted from you to the air. It's so gradual, you're not aware of the interchange. But you are very conscious of conduction when you walk barefoot on a tile floor. Your feet feel icy immediately. That's because tile is a very good heat conductor; heat moves quickly from your feet to the tile. Wood is a much poorer conductor, so you're more comfortable walking on a wooden floor. Carpets conduct heat very poorly. So cover a tiled bathroom floor with a carpet or a mat, and you won't feel icy when you step on it.

Remember, things get cold because they lose heat. Your feet get cold because they lose heat to the tile—heat is conducted away. When you pick up a glass of ice water, your hand feels cold because heat goes from it to the glass. Metals are also good heat conductors. So at least in one way, wooden ski poles are preferable to metal ones. Wood is a much poorer heat conductor, so your hands don't get so cold as they would if you were using metal poles. But metal poles are usually supplied with rubber grips. Skiers prefer metal poles because metal is much lighter than wood, and the grips cut down heat loss.

You lose heat by radiation, conduction, and convection. You gain it in those ways also. In addition, you lose heat by evaporation. To keep warm, you must reduce these factors, or as many of them as possible. This is true no matter where you may be—indoors, outdoors, moving about or resting in bed; even in outer space. No group does this better than the Eskimos, Laplanders, and other people who live in the far north.

3/ Eskimos Keep Warm— Desert Dwellers

Keep Cool

Your body is remarkably able to maintain a normal temperature, especially deep inside you. When the air temperature drops, even as much as 25°, the temperature change inside you may be only a degree, or less. However, under the same conditions skin temperature changes a lot more. It is very sensitive to temperature changes. In fact, doctors tell us that a small area in the center of the forehead can detect air temperature changes as small as a hundredth of a degree.

As we mentioned in the last chapter, people lose much heat by evaporation of moisture. A marathon runner or boxer—anyone who sweats a lot—loses a tremendous amount of heat by evaporation. Such athletes lose so much water that their body weight may drop several pounds. But they get back the pounds as soon as they drink water to replace the amount they lost.

People who live in hot desert regions need protection from the hot, dry daytime air. Without it, even though they may not perspire, their bodies would release large amounts of water—the dry air would take it from them.

Desert dwellers wear loose-fitting robes, often with hoods to cover their heads and frequently made of light woolen cloth. The robe keeps heat from getting to them, and it also reflects sunlight away from them. At the same time, moisture from their bodies is trapped inside the robes. A person wearing such a robe is surrounded by moist air, and this slows down the loss of additional water.

A desert dweller's problems are two-fold: keeping from getting too warm, and keeping from losing too much water. The problems of Eskimos and Laplanders, people who live in the far north, are quite different. They are concerned with *saving* body heat, and being sure they do not get so hot that they perspire.

In far northern latitudes of North America, where Eskimos live, and in the far north of Eurasia, the land of the Laplanders, temperatures often drop to 60° below zero. And the wind blows just about all the time. Should it be blowing at 30 miles an hour, the temperature on any skin exposed to it would feel like 140° below zero. Without a lot of protection, and the right kind of protection, no one can survive such temperatures for more than a few minutes.

No people live in Antarctica except scientists and workmen who have been sent there. The weather conditions they have to put up with are just as bad as, and often worse than, those that occur in northern latitudes. People who work at the Antarctic stations refer to what they call the 30-30-30 Rule for Survival: When exposed to a temperature of minus 30° and winds of 30 miles an hour, human flesh freezes solid in 30 seconds. Eskimos, Laplanders, and Antarctic scientists are often exposed to such conditions, but they survive them.

One reason they keep warm is that their bodies generate more heat than yours does. They "burn" food faster. We say they have a higher basal metabolism—the rate the body changes food into useful energy. This is probably because they eat a lot of meat (protein and fat), almost a pound a day.

Tests were made by the U.S. Army when it was training soldiers for survival in cold regions. They found that when Eskimos changed their diet and ate the food soldiers were receiving, their basal metabolism fell rapidly. At the same time, it was found that if soldiers ate more meat, their basal metabolism went up. In only three days, they were burning food as fast as the meat-eating Eskimos.

A way of saving heat is to reduce body surface as much as possible. When it's very cold, you pull your knees up to your chest. And as you go to sleep, you may wrap your arms around your legs, making yourself into a ball.

What you're doing is decreasing the amount of body surface from which you lose heat. Natives of the far north do this also. In addition, they have smaller bodies, especially the hands and feet. It seems that over the thousands of years they have lived in cold climates, the bodies of northerners have changed so they can better survive the cold. Not only are their hands and feet smaller, but the blood vessels inside them are able to widen considerably. Because of the greater width, more blood can pass through the hands and feet. The extra blood supplies them with an increased amount of heat.

Eskimos can work outside with bare hands at temperatures much colder than you could stand. But they wear mittens to keep their hands dry. Should they get wet, they dry their hands at once. Remember that evaporation causes cooling; it drops skin temperature several degrees below the temperature of the air. As it gets colder, northerners wear boots and mittens—always mittens, and not gloves. With mittens, the exposed surface of the hand is made smaller, and the fingers touch one another and heat each other by conduction.

People of the far north eat food that produces a lot of heat. And once their bodies generate the heat, they have learned how to keep from losing it. They know how to keep warm by eating meat, by wearing the proper kind of clothing, and by building the right kind of shelter.

Shelters

Laplanders live where there is a lot of wood. So their shelters are often made of logs. Snow is piled high around them to keep out the wind. However, Laplanders are nomads. So much of the time they move about. They have to, because they depend upon reindeer for clothing, and also for much of their shelter and food. Huge herds, sometimes numbering several thousand, move across the land in search of food. The Laplanders must follow. When roving, which is most of the time, the Laplanders leave their log homes and build shelters out of animal skins supported on wooden poles. What they do, in effect, is make a skin tent. When several layers are used, and snow or dried grass is packed around and between them, the shelters can be kept comfortable. If you have ever done cold-weather camping, you know that even a thin tent can be kept warm. In the first place, the tent is no larger than necessary. It is completely closed except for a small opening for fresh air. Body heat is trapped inside. In addition, the heat from only a small heater is needed—sometimes a single candle is adequate.

CONSTRUCTING A WHALE RIB AND SOD SHELTER

Animal skin

hay or sod

caribou skin

whale rib

sod

The Eskimos of North America also used animal skins to make shelters. In fact, just about everything the Eskimos had—their food, tools, clothing, and shelter—came from animals such as whales and seals, as well as from fish and birds. (We say "had" because many Eskimos live differently today. Modern ways have been introduced as the area has been developed to get oil out of the ground and to harness rivers for huge electric power plants.)

Eskimos who lived along the coast used to use whale bones to make the frames of their shelters. Then they covered the frames with animal skins, such as those of caribou, as they call the deer of the north. Dried grass was laid over that skin and another animal skin was placed over the grass. (Grass is a good insulator, serving the same purpose that glass wool serves in your house.) Snow was piled around the "tent" and also piled on the outer skin.

It was protection from the wind, and it was also another insulator. Shrubs in your garden can withstand severe winters if snow is packed around them. The snow keeps them from losing heat.

Eskimo shelters had no doors or flaps, such as those you use in your tent, or like the ones Indians used in their teepees. Instead, Eskimos entered by crawling through a long tunnel that sloped upward to the shelter. The slope was important because it served to trap the warm air inside.

Cold air is heavier than warm air. It therefore tends to move downward, and the lighter warm air tends to "float" on top of the colder air. The cold air could not move upward into the shelter, and the warm air could not move down the tunnel; it was trapped. One danger with such an arrangement was that the air might become stale and unfit to breathe. But the Eskimos knew how to

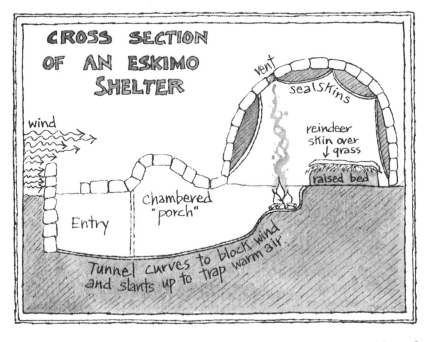

CROSS SECTION OF AN ESKIMO SHELTER

wind

vent

sealskins

reindeer skin over ↓ grass

raised bed

chambered "porch"

Entry

Tunnel curves to block wind and slants up to trap warm air.

avoid that. As people moved through the passage they pushed fresh air into the shelter. And the stale air moved out through small vents.

These houses of bone, animal skins, and grass were surprisingly warm. Oil lamps were used for cooking food. When the lamps were lit, the temperature went so high that the people had to take off their outer layers of clothing. Even then, they were often too hot to be comfortable. At night when the lamps had been put out, the temperature inside the shelter dropped to about 60°. That was warm enough for people to sleep under light animal-skin blankets. Their beds were hard, since they were made of stone blocks covered with a layer of dried grass. Skins of reindeer were laid over the grass. The floor was the coldest part of a shelter; it was slightly warmer at the level of the raised platform bed.

Many north-country people lived far from the sea, and in places that had no trees, so they had no whale bones or sticks to support their structures. But there was plenty of snow, so that became their building material.

Igloos

You may have built a snow house by digging an opening in a snowbank. Igloos were snow houses, but they were not dug out of the snow. They were built of blocks of snow—the snow wasn't light and fluffy; it was packed hard enough to hold its shape. Because the snow was packed, the blocks cut out of the snow could be large—as large as 3 feet long, 2 feet wide and 6 or 8 inches thick. The first layer made a circle the size of the finished igloo. The blocks in the second layer were placed slightly inside

BUILDING AN IGLOO

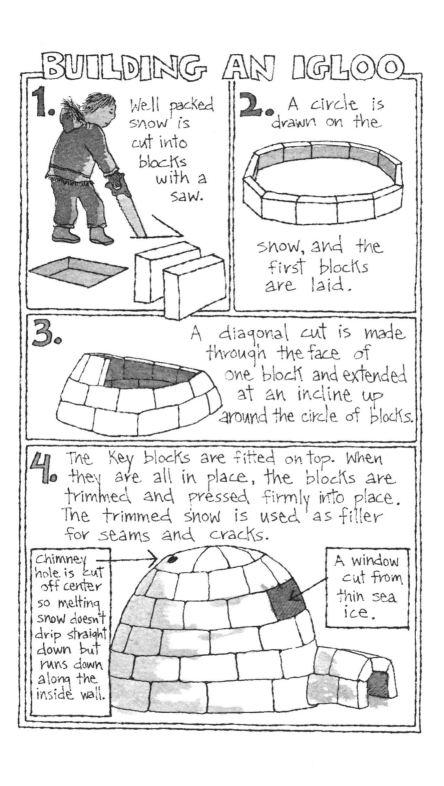

1. Well packed snow is cut into blocks with a saw.

2. A circle is drawn on the snow, and the first blocks are laid.

3. A diagonal cut is made through the face of one block and extended at an incline up around the circle of blocks.

4. The key blocks are fitted on top. When they are all in place, the blocks are trimmed and pressed firmly into place. The trimmed snow is used as filler for seams and cracks.

Chimney hole is cut off center so melting snow doesn't drip straight down but runs down along the inside wall.

A window cut from thin sea ice.

the first layer. And so it went, layer upon layer. A hunter who needed a shelter for the night could cut out the snow blocks and build an igloo in less than an hour. Of course, it was a small igloo, only large enough for the hunter. However, entire families often lived in an igloo. This one had to be bigger, sometimes 15 feet across and 7 or 8 feet high. And it would even have a window or two. Slabs of clear ice were set into the wall. They let in light but prevented the loss of heat. There were windows in the igloo but no doors. Just a passageway. You remember that entry to the skin tents was through a tunnel. The same was true with the igloos. The passage sloped up to the igloo so cold air acted as a seal against the loss of warm air. Movement through the passage agitated the air enough to force "new" air into the igloo. A small opening at the top of the shelter was a vent for stale air, and for the smoke given off by an oil cooking lamp.

A person could keep very warm inside an igloo because snow is a good insulator. Even when snow is packed, there are spaces throughout. These dead air spaces slow the movement of heat. In Maine and other cold parts of our country, many people pack snow around their houses. It keeps the houses warmer.

One trouble with igloos was that they often became too warm. Because of the heat given off by people inside of it, the temperature in an igloo would go up to about 40° without anyone's lighting a fire or burning a lamp. When a lamp was lit, the temperature would go much higher—high enough to melt the snow and cause the walls to drip.

In the large igloos used by entire families, melting was prevented by lining the inside of the shelter with animal skins, usually sealskins. The skins were insulators that kept inside heat from reaching the snow walls.

The temperature inside these igloos would go to 70°, so warm that people inside were uncomfortable. At night when the cooking lamp was out, the temperature dropped to a more pleasant level. Eskimos slept on snow beds. Blocks of snow were built up to make a sleeping platform. Since it was raised above the floor, the air there was warmer. To prevent loss of body heat to the snow, the platform was covered with several layers of animal skins. And the same kind of skins were used as blankets.

The Eskimos were good engineers. Even though they probably had never heard about radiation, convection, and conduction, they knew how to regulate and control the movement of heat from one place to another. Their shelters were marvels of heat conservation, and so was their clothing.

Cold-Weather Clothing

Clothing must keep northerners warm. But it cannot be heavy because the people need to move quickly and quietly. The ideal clothing is made of animal skin. The skin side (leather) makes a fine shield against the wind. (Leather coats and jackets are also worn today by Russians and other people who live in severely cold parts of the world.) Caribou skins are especially effective in holding heat. For one thing, each hair is hollow, so it contains dead air—one of the best insulators. (A deer can lie in a snow bed without its body heat melting any of the snow.) Also, each hair is wider at the tip than it is at the base. The wide tips of the hairs fit together tightly, making a sort of roof that traps air between the "roof" and the skin surface. Once again there is dead-air insulation.

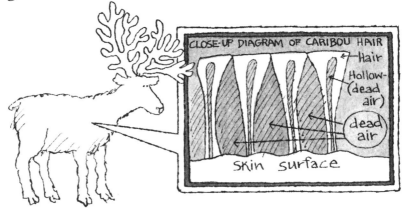

CLOSE-UP DIAGRAM OF CARIBOU HAIR
Hair
Hollow (dead air)
dead air
Skin surface

Perhaps you've noticed that two or three layers of light clothing keep you warmer than a single heavy layer does. Long ago the Eskimos knew this was true. They wore two layers of animal skins. The inner skin was turned so the hair side faced them; the outer skin layer had the hair facing the outside. The skins fit very loosely, so a person kept warm and dry. Air could move and water could evaporate.

FASHION TIP: When it's cold and windy..... Wear your mink coat inside out! It's warmer!

The fit of the clothing was as important as the type. It had to be loose so air could move, so loose that people could slide their arms out of the sleeves and bring their hands (still inside their clothing) up to their faces and rub them. It even had to be loose enough for a person

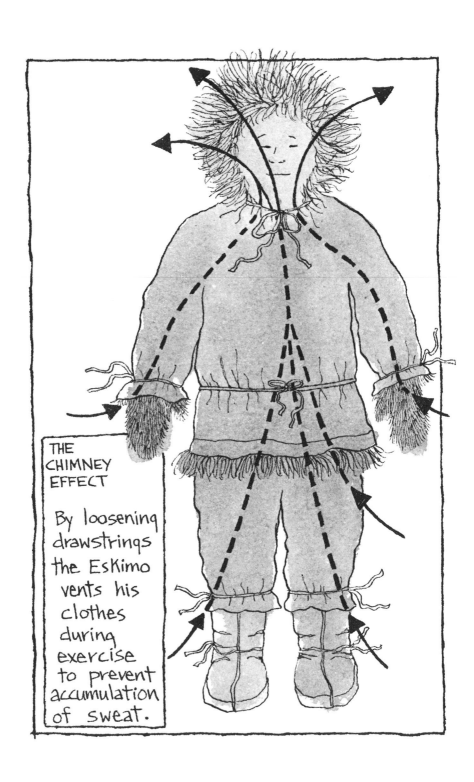

THE
CHIMNEY
EFFECT

By loosening
drawstrings
the Eskimo
vents his
clothes
during
exercise
to prevent
accumulation
of sweat.

to turn around inside it. The hood or parka was so large it extended far beyond the face. The only time the wind could hit a person was when it came directly from the front.

Animal skins made good clothing, but they were pretty smelly. The skins were cured with the urine of animals, and when the skins got warm, as they did inside the warm igloos, a person became well aware of how the curing had been accomplished.

Inside their animal skins Eskimos could keep warm even when the temperature was a 100° below zero. Body heat was trapped, keeping the person surrounded by warm, humid air, just about as warm and humid as the air in the tropical islands of the Caribbean.

An ever-present danger in severely cold regions is moisture. Perspiration must be avoided, for when it evaporates, it removes heat rapidly. Clothing must also be kept dry at all times. The effectiveness of most insulators drops quickly when they are wet. Water replaces the dead air. Eskimos were fanatics about keeping dry; they had to be in order to survive. Before entering an igloo they carefully brushed off any snow, and knocked it off their boots. Once inside, their clothing was hung over the cooking lamps to dry it out.

Anyone who has to spend time outside during the cold weather would be smart to do the same thing. Clothing must be kept dry. It must allow body moisture to evaporate gradually, and yet prevent rain or snow from entering. Several light layers are much more effective than a single heavier layer. Also, layers can then be added or subtracted as the weather changes. The clothing should include woolen underwear and a woolen sweater or shirt. Also,

woolen headgear. That's especially important. The brain needs oxygen and heat in order to function, so the supply of blood to the brain cannot be decreased, even though the body may be conserving heat. As a result, as much as half of one's body heat can be lost through the head and neck.

Strange as it seems, wearing a hat can keep your hands and feet warm. Your hat stops the loss of large amounts of body heat, and so your body can afford to send more of that heat to other parts of your body. When your head is cold, your hands and feet get colder and colder, because your body's first need is to keep the brain warm; so that's where the heat goes.

One of the best insulators for winter clothing is down. When it is fluffed, a large amount of dead air is trapped. That's why ducks, geese, and other birds can endure severely cold winters. They have down to protect them. They have other ways of keeping warm, too.

4 / Birds in Winter

You don't see many birds in winter. Many have left your area, and those that remain are struggling to keep warm. They are less active, because activity uses energy that is needed to keep warm. The most severe problems for birds in winter are getting enough heat and holding on to the heat once it is generated. These are problems for all birds, but especially for very small ones.

Small birds have a harder time than large ones because they have a large surface area (from which heat is lost) relative to their volume.

Two balls or spheres may help you understand the relationship of volume to surface better. Suppose there were two spheres, one having a radius of 10 inches and the other a radius 10 times greater, or 100 inches. The volume of the second sphere will be 1000 times greater than the volume of the smaller sphere. But the surface of the larger sphere will be only 100 times greater. If the two objects were birds rather than spheres, the larger bird would have a volume 1000 times that of the smaller bird, so it could produce 1000 times more energy. But its surface area would be only 100 times greater. It would make 1000 times more energy, yet it would lose only 100 times more.

The big bird would be able to conserve more heat; it would be easier for it to keep warm.

Small birds have a hard time staying alive during winter months. Many small birds die during winter either because they cannot find enough food or because the weather remains so cold for so long that they cannot eat enough to keep alive, even though they have many ways of fighting the cold.

You remember we mentioned earlier that you shiver to keep warm. The heat that you generate is produced mostly in your muscles, and the muscles produce more heat when they are active. So one way of keeping warm is to move about, use your muscles. Another way is to shiver. When your body needs heat, the muscles tighten and loosen rapidly—they become active. Just as you shiver to keep warm, so do birds.

When it's icy cold—the air is cold and the wind is blowing—temperatures go down and down. When it's 10° below zero and the wind is blowing 30 miles an hour, the temperature feels like 63° below zero. Still air may be very cold, but the wind makes air seem even colder. In some parts of the country this wind chilling causes temperatures to seem as though it were 60° and 70° below zero.

Yet birds survive. They keep alive by eating, and by shivering—they shiver without stopping. They just perch and shiver, making as much heat as possible and remaining still so they use as little as possible. Shivering enables a bird to make four or five times more heat than it would make if it were not shivering. It has been found that when the temperature is as low as 94° below zero, some birds can keep their body temperature at 104° for several hours. About the only times birds leave a perch is to seek more food. Shivering is only one way that birds keep alive during an icy blast. Another is by reducing the amount of heat they require.

You and I are not able to do this. Regardless of weather conditions, you need to keep your body temperature at 98.6°, or very close to it. When a bird is active, its body temperature is 104°, higher than your temperature. But when a bird is inactive, as during sleep, its body temperature drops. All its life processes slow down, so the bird can survive even when its temperature has dropped some 20 degrees, to about 84°. Birds, especially very small ones, can store up only a small amount of food; their bodies aren't large enough to hold much. So one way of stretching the limited supply is to decrease temperature; lower temperatures mean that food is used more slowly. These small birds have the ability to "turn up the thermostat" at dawn. Their body functions increase rapidly, and within a few minutes their body temperature is once more at 104°, and the bird becomes active.

Even though birds shiver to make more heat, and drop their temperature so less heat is required, they must still conserve whatever heat they have. One way they do this is by increasing their insulation. Just as we add clothing during winter, and change the kind of clothing we wear, so do birds. They grow more feathers. And many of the feathers they grow are the small underfeathers, the down that grows beneath the large outer feathers. This is one of the best of all insulators. Jackets filled with down are light, but very warm. A down-filled blanket, or comforter, makes you comfortable in bed because it is light, and it keeps you from losing much heat. The down is able to trap air. A down-covered bird loses very little heat. As the temperature drops, birds fluff their feathers. They trap greater amounts of air among the down feathers. They hunch on a limb, remain still, and so can keep quite comfortable even when temperatures may be well below zero.

Often you can't see the birds unless you look for them. They don't perch out in the open. Birds seek out a place that protects them from the wind and storm. A favorite perch is on the inner branches of pine trees. There they are surrounded by the needles, so the wind doesn't strike them. Also, the protected spot prevents heat loss by radiation. Remember that heat moves by radiation from a warm surface to one that is cooler. This process goes on rapidly when the warm surface is open to the sky. When the heat source is closed in somewhat, as it is when a bird is surrounded by pine needles, radiation is slower.

When there is not much snow, birds can find food such as seeds. But those that eat insects, like woodpeckers, have a hard time. And all birds must search widely when the ground is snow covered. If you happen to live in the country, it's a good idea to put out seeds for the birds, and pieces of fat for the insect eaters. That's especially true when the temperature is low, because birds cannot afford

plastic front keeps out larger birds

Orange slices attract cardinals

Bird feeder with sunflower seed, sunflower + peanut hearts, white millet + red millet

Thistle seed feeder attracts goldfinches and other small birds

suet (in onion bag) for woodpeckers, nuthatches and other insect eaters

Mixed seed and cracked corn for larger birds and ground feeders

to spend a lot of energy searching for food. If they can get food quickly, as they can at a feeder, they can keep warmer. Also, if there is plenty of food, the birds can eat their fill and so have enough food inside them to last several hours.

Although many birds are lost during cold weather, many survive because they fluff their feathers, drop their body temperature, shiver, and are lucky enough to find lots of food. They know how to keep warm, even when it is icy cold. And so do many animals, especially black bears.

5/ Black Bears

in Winter

Unlike birds that must fight winter's chill, black bears escape it as much as they can. In winter they take a long sleep, nestled deep inside a small cave or a hollow tree. Even though the temperature may drop to 30° or 40° below zero, a bear keeps warm.

As soon as spring brings a new growth of bushes and berries, bears start feeding. They eat and eat. All through the spring and summer their feeding continues. The bears build themselves up, storing food and fats that will be needed in the fall when they start their long sleep. As the days grow shorter, and the temperature begins to fall, bears hunt for a sleeping place. It may be a shallow cave, or simply a deep crevice between rocks. If a hollowed-out log is available, chances are a bear will end up occupying it. Logs seem to be their favorite locations. Bears tend to choose small spaces. They can keep warmer in a cave that's just large enough to hold them than in a larger cave. They usually line their sleeping place with leaves and with dried grass, if it is available. No food is stored in the cave, for all through their winter naps, bears will not eat. Often they will sleep for 7 months, stirring only occasionally. During that time they neither eat nor drink. And they have no apparent way to get rid of wastes. For as much as 7 months they neither urinate nor defecate—get rid of solid wastes.

Bears don't go into a coma, however. They can be roused. And very often the females will give birth to cubs sometime in January. They have to be somewhat active to do that and to provide warm milk for the newborn cubs. (The cubs do not hibernate, but they sleep a great deal. About all they do is nurse and sleep. When they defecate, the mother bears use their waste as food.)

A mother bear is producing milk, so for that reason alone, her body must be active to some degree. Her body temperature, therefore, cannot drop very low. And it doesn't. Normally a bear's body temperature is about 100°. During its winter sleep this temperature drops only about 12 degrees. That temperature is maintained almost entirely by using fats stored in its body. It's a wonder that bears can do this, even when the temperature may be way below zero.

They are able to keep warm for reasons you already know about. They are inactive, so just about all their energy goes toward keeping warm. Even their heart rate goes way down. When a bear is walking about and feeding, its heart beats between 50 and 90 times—the more active, the faster the rate. During the long winter sleep, it's not unusual for the heart to beat only 8 times a minute, just enough to keep the blood circulating. Should a bear be roused a bit, it might lift its head and look around in a dazed sort of way. Then the heart rate would increase somewhat. And the heart must beat faster when the bear gives birth to her cubs.

Because of the slowdown in body needs, bears can produce enough heat to keep warm. But once the heat is generated, it must be preserved. In other words, bears must be well insulated. It helps that their sleeping places are lined with leaves and grass. Also, as winter approaches, new growths of hair appear. The hair comes in thick and full, and when the bear fluffs it up, air is trapped between the hairs and between the outer surface of the hair and the skin of the animal. You remember that dead air is a very good insulator.

Another way bears conserve heat is to reduce their body surface as much as possible. Bears curl up, making themselves into a ball, just as you do when you're cold. They poke their noses into their bellies and hold that position. A smaller body surface exposed to the air means a smaller loss of heat.

Black bears don't attempt to fight winter's weather. Instinct causes them to fatten in spring and summer, seek out snug sleeping places, line them with leaves and grass, curl up, slow down their body processes, and wait until spring brings forth new boughs, leaves, and berries.

Humans cannot escape winter so easily. They can't snuggle in for a winter nap that covers several months. However, people have learned how to endure winter by building tight houses that hold the heat they put into them. They have learned to eat an energy-giving diet and to wear clothing that slows the loss of body heat.

6/Heating Our Houses

While you're reading this book, you are warm and snug. At least we hope you are. But if you had lived in America around the time of the Pilgrims, it would be a different story. You might be warm if you were sitting in front of the fireplace, or even sitting inside the fireplace—some of them were so big that more than one person could do so. But if you were sitting in any other part of the house you would be wrapped in heavy clothing; you would probably be wearing boots, a hat, and mittens. And even then you might shiver occasionally. Near the fire it was warm, but anywhere else it was cold.

Early houses were often built of green wood; they had to be, for there wasn't time for the wood to dry. As green wood dries, it shrinks. So even though the boards would fit well when the house was built, they often shrank enough for cracks to develop. The cracks had to be stuffed with dried grass. Where they weren't, the wind would blow through, and it was not unusual during storms for piles of snow to build up on the floor. Colonial houses were cold and drafty.

The only heat in those houses was from the fireplace that was used for cooking as well as heat; stoves had not yet been invented. Fireplaces burn a lot of wood, but they are poor house heaters. In those days, the only way heat got into the house was by radiation. You remember, this is the way heat moves from something hot to something that is cooler.

When people sat in front of a fireplace, the front of them became warm by radiation. But their backs were icy. No heat could reach their backs by radiation, and the air in the room was heated very little. The same thing happens with a campfire—your front gets hot but your back stays cold. That's why fireplaces were made very large: People could get close to the fire, and the bricks and stones inside the fireplace became warm, radiating heat to the people sitting there.

People got warm by sitting inside the fireplace. At the same time, however, tremendous amounts of air went up the chimney. The air was heated somewhat by the fire, but as fast as it was heated, it went up the chimney. In larger houses, the only way to keep at all warm was to have a fireplace in each room. Even then, people had to be hardy to withstand winter's cold.

Many of today's houses have fireplaces built in. Perhaps there's one in your house. If it is an ordinary fireplace, it's no more efficient than the ones built long ago. Actually, such fireplaces remove more heat from a house than they put into it. Air heated in other ways, by a furnace for example, moves toward the fire, and it goes up the chimney. The fireplace takes away warm air. The next time you light the fireplace, notice what happens in the rest of the room. If there's a thermostat that controls your furnace, very likely the heat will come on. In many houses, however, the fireplace is built in such a way that it does not remove heat from the room; some even add heat.

One way of doing this is by feeding outside air to the fire through a duct in the floor of the fireplace. The air (oxygen) needed to keep the fire burning then comes from outside the house; it is heated and then goes up the chimney. The movement of inside air toward the fireplace is reduced. That amount can be cut down by using the duct together with glass doors mounted in the fireplace opening. They virtually stop the loss of air from the room. But they slow down radiation, so less heat gets into the room by that process.

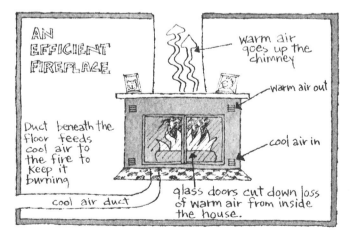

Another scheme to make fireplaces into heaters uses a double-walled metal insert. It becomes the core of the fireplace, and bricks or stones are built around this unit. The fire heats the air between the two walls of the unit, which has openings at the bottom and the top. Cool air enters through the bottom vents. It is heated and released into the room through the upper vents. The fireplace becomes an air circulator. When such a unit is used together with a duct that supplies outside air for the burning of the fire, the efficiency of the fireplace goes up. But it is still a poor way to heat a house. Most of the effect of a fireplace is what you see; it makes people feel warmer when they see a crackling fire.

Early settlers in America had no such luxuries in their fireplaces. They realized, however, that the huge, sit-in "cooking" fireplaces didn't keep a house warm. That's why they made fireplaces smaller and built separate fireplaces in several rooms of the house.

That's the way American houses were heated for over a hundred years. In the late 1700s stoves were invented. They were a tremendous improvement. Imagine how much easier it became to cook a meal. Pots could be placed on a stove top where there was now steady and even heat. And the stoves were also efficient room heaters. Heat radiated from them. In addition, air touching the stove became heated by conduction. The warm air moved upward from the stove and cooler air moved along the floor toward the stove; convection currents were set up. So heat was distributed in several different ways. Also, only a small amount of air from the room, just enough to keep the fire burning, went up the chimney.

But a stove heated only one room, or one section of a

house. The rest of the house was freezing cold. In winter many families closed parts of their houses, and everyone lived in those rooms that got some heat from the stove. At bedtime, people washed up and put on night clothes close to the stove, then made a quick dash into the cold bed. If they were lucky, the mattress was filled with feathers (a feather bed) so they sank into it and it came up around them. Often a down-filled comforter covered the feather mattress. The room was so chilled that people could see their breath, and their ears tingled with the cold. So they curled up as much as possible. Sometimes they wore night-caps to slow down loss of heat from their heads. Body heat was conserved and soon it warmed the bed. The feathers above and below were such good insulators a person was snug throughout the night, even though on the floor there might be piles of snow that drifted in through cracks and crevices.

WARMING PAN

If you were especially favored, the bed might have been prewarmed. Bricks that had been placed near the stove were wrapped in cloths and then put inside the covers to warm the foot of the bed. Instead of bricks, some families used a long-handled warming pan. This was a flat, round pan with a lid on it. Hot coals from the fire were placed inside the pan. The lid was closed, and then the hot pan was moved around inside the blankets.

Central heating, which made bed warming unnecessary, was to follow in the next few decades. Among the first devices were wood furnaces in the cellar. Air from the house went to the furnace through a cold-air return. The air circulated through the furnace and was returned to the house through a hot-air register, usually located in the central part of the house.

These single-register furnaces were a great improvement over room stoves. But parts of the house far from the register were still cold. Gradually furnaces were fitted with ducts that carried hot air from the furnace to each of the rooms. The air moved by convection. Cold air entered at the bottom of the furnace. It was heated, and the warmed air moved into the house through the ducts.

At the close of the 19th century, when electric motors became available, fans were put into the system. These pushed the air along, moving it faster than convection alone would take it. And so there was forced hot-air heating, a method that is used today in a good many homes.

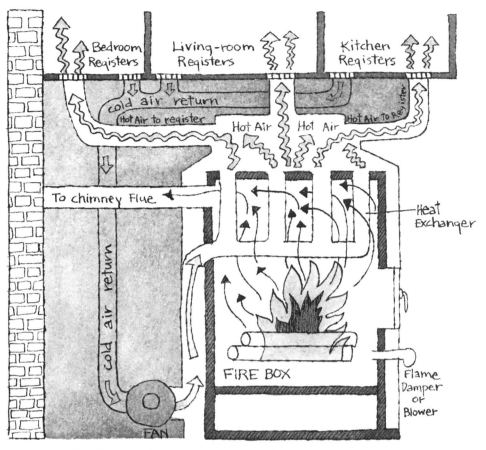

Bedroom Registers

Living-room Registers

Kitchen Registers

cold air return

Hot Air to register

Hot Air

Hot Air

Hot Air To Register

To chimney Flue

Heat Exchanger

cold air return

FIRE BOX

Flame Damper or Blower

FAN

A TYPICAL WOOD FURNACE

It is the best system for people who have hay fever, or have trouble breathing for other reasons. In addition to heating the air that goes through the house, the system can change the air in other ways. The air can go through a filter that removes dust, ash, and also the pollen grains that bother many people. Also, the air can be dried if necessary, or moisture can be added to it. Usually during winter, humidity is lower in our houses than it should be. Dry air causes many people to develop coughs. Humidity should be about 50%, and a forced air system can easily maintain that level. Also, air conditioning can be added to the system with little trouble and at a minimum cost. In summer air can be cooled, and then circulated through the entire house using the same ducts that carry hot air during the winter.

Air can be used to move heat through a house; so can steam or water.

In a hot-water system, the furnace heats water in a boiler. Pipes go from the boiler to radiators located in each of the rooms, usually beneath a window. Convection moves the water through the system, although in most cases electric pumps also move the water along.

Heat radiates into the room through the radiators. Also, air touching them becomes hot. It rises past the windows to the ceiling, cools somewhat, and falls at the opposite end of the room. So the entire room is heated. The cooled water returns to the furnace, where it is reheated and then recirculated.

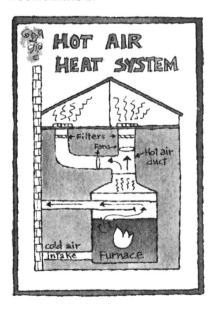

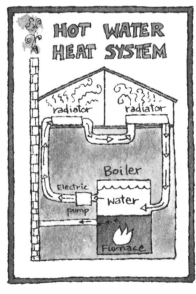

In high apartment houses, hotels, office buildings, and other large structures, hot-air and hot-water systems would not work. The air or water would cool long before it reached all parts of the building. Also, water could not be used because pressure would have to be too high to push along the tremendous amount there would have to be in the system. The only reasonable way of heating large buildings is with steam. Very hot steam expands through the pipes and radiators, heating them and the rooms where they are located. As the steam cools, it condenses into water, which then flows downward toward the furnace through the same pipes.

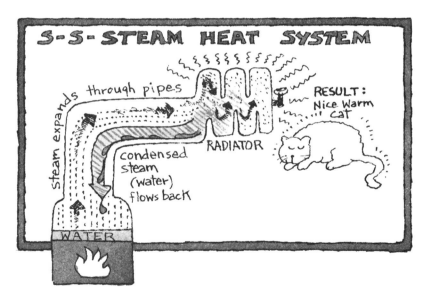

Even if the New England settlers had had central heating, their houses still would have been cold. You remember they were built out of green lumber that shrank as it dried. Windows did not fit tightly, so that was another way heat was lost. There was no insulation, so there was no way the houses could hold heat. Even today a heating

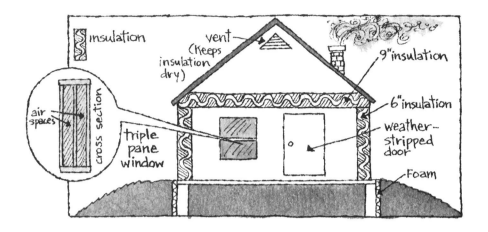

system cannot keep a house warm unless the house is well insulated, and there are few if any cracks where heat can escape.

Heat is lost through windows, so houses must have storm sashes—double or triple windows with dead-air spaces between them. All cracks must be filled, and houses must be insulated. They must be surrounded on top, sides, and bottom with materials that contain dead-air spaces—plastic foam, rock wool, glass wool. The insulating material must not pick up moisture, and it must not be something that appeals to mice or other rodents as a nesting place. Also, it must not pack together.

When a house is well built and well insulated, and contains a good heating system, you can be very comfortable in it. But even the best-made houses must burn fuel, and all kinds of fuel have become very expensive. In the early 1970s oil was three dollars a barrel. A few years ago it was $36 a barrel, more than 1000% higher. People who used to heat their houses for $300 dollars a winter had to spend more than $3000. The price varies, but it remains very high.

The furnaces we mentioned above—hot air, water, or steam—may burn either oil or gas. Gas has been less expensive than oil in most locations. But the price will rise rapidly to equal that of oil.

Where wood is cheap many people are changing their furnaces to wood-burning ones. But not everyone can do this; it is hard work to cut wood, and a wood fire needs lots of attention. With oil or gas all you need do to get heat is turn up the thermostat. As more wood is used, even wood will become expensive. Where it is plentiful, a cord of wood costs about $60. (A cord is a pile that measures 4 feet by 4 feet and is 8 feet long. Some people say it should be stacked tight enough so that a mouse might get through it, but not the cat chasing the mouse.) In some cities, and even in country places where wood is scarce, a cord costs 3 times as much.

People have developed ways of keeping their houses warm, and they have all kinds of furnaces and heating systems. They can burn wood or coal in stoves to reduce the amount of gas or oil that they have to buy. And they know how to make their houses heat-tight. But keeping warm inside a house will cost more and more as fuels become more expensive. So people must insulate more and must get used to lower temperatures: 68° in daytime, and 60° at night.

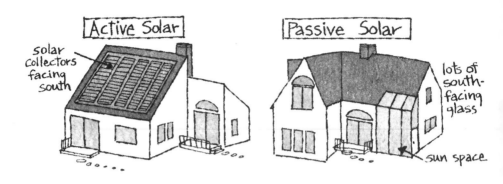

Solar and Electric Houses

You can keep warm for less money by living in a passive solar house that is designed to catch sunlight and convert it into heat. Windows on the south side of a house become heat traps on a sunny day, even when it's very cold outside. A well-designed greenhouse also catches sunlight on the south side. The inside wall of the greenhouse may be built of stone or concrete, or it may be a wall of water containers, and the floor may be brick or stone. All of these pick up heat and hold it long after the sun has set.

An active solar house is one that contains solar collectors—hot water or hot air—which are usually mounted on the roof. Pumps circulate the water or air through the collectors and distribute it to various parts of the house. In those parts of the world that have abundant sunshine, solar energy is very effective in space heating.

You've probably heard people say how great it would be if we could can the heat of summer and save it until winter when it is needed. Well, it is being done. An experimental house that recycles heat—uses it over and over again—is now being tested. During the summer, heat is collected from outside and from inside the house and is carried to a large tank of water. The tank can be in the basement, or located under the yard or driveway. Heat is added all during the summer, raising the temperature high enough for the heat to be used to warm the house. In winter, water pipes inside the tank pick up summer's heat and carry it to all parts of the house. The system cools the house in summer and heats it in winter. No fuel is burned. The only power needed is electricity to run the circulator pumps. It sounds like a good idea, and it may work where winters are not too severe. A lot of

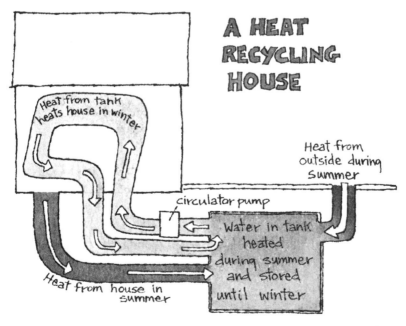

A HEAT RECYCLING HOUSE

Heat from tank heats house in winter

Heat from outside during summer

circulator pump

Water in tank heated during summer and stored until winter

Heat from house in summer

money would be needed to install the system, but it would be inexpensive to operate.

There are engineers who believe that eventually people's homes will be heated by electricity—perhaps using the electricity to run heat pumps that collect heat from outside and concentrate it inside. The action is much the same as a refrigerator which takes heat from inside the box and puts it into the kitchen. Even on a cold day, outside air contains some heat. A heat pump collects the heat from a large volume of air and concentrates it in the house. In summer the process is reversed. The heat pump takes heat from inside the house and puts it outside.

These engineers believe that oil and coal, and gas, too, should not, and eventually will not, be burned as fuels. Rather they should be used only as raw materials for the chemical industry. Somewhere along the line hundreds of thousands of products such as plastics, synthetic fabrics, medicines, and fertilizers use chemicals provided by coal, gas, or oil. Rather than burning these fuels to produce the electricity, it will come from nuclear fusion, from solar-electric generators, and from hydropower. Many engineers believe, however, that nuclear fusion is the final answer to the world's energy needs. It is the basic process that produces the energy of the universe, of the sun and other stars. In a fusion reaction, hydrogen is the fuel, and the supply of hydrogen is endless.

Tremendous problems must be solved before the fusion reaction can be brought under control. Engineers through-out the world are working to find ways to solve them. Some believe that if we make an all-out effort, it will be possible to generate electricity by nuclear fusion before the end of this century, or early in the 21st century.

Should that happen, electricity would be cheap and plentiful. Meanwhile people must keep warm in other, and more expensive, ways and get into the habit of wearing the kind of clothing that conserves heat.

7/Clothes Keep

Us Warm

Your body easily produces enough heat to keep you warm as long as the temperature goes no lower than about 75°. As the temperature drops, you can produce additional heat, but there are limits to it. It becomes essential to conserve heat—to prevent the loss of heat once it has been generated.

One way is to grow a thick head of hair. Often half of the heat you lose is lost through your head. Large amounts of blood and heat are supplied to the brain. And there is very little flesh on your head to hold the heat. Put on a hat and you'll feel warmer—not only your head but also your hands and feet. When your ancestors were living in unheated houses, they often wore nightcaps when they went to bed. It was a good idea. Your body may be snug under the blankets, but your head will be giving off a lot of heat. A cap helps hold it in. A nightcap keeps your feet warm.

A cap that traps air is best, just as clothing that traps air is best for the rest of your body. You remember that we mentioned earlier that down is the most effective heat holder. It is light and contains a tremendous number of dead-air spaces. But it is expensive. Recently several synthetic products have been made which are cheaper and quite effective. Two of these are very thin, crinkly fibers called Polarguard and Thermolactyl. You may see the names on labels of cold-weather clothing. The most widely used fiber for winter is wool. The fibers are crinkly, and so lock together when made into yarn. Also, they do not pack, and so remain fluffy.

Recently people who design warm clothing have become interested in polar bears. You think of them as white. But when their hair was studied carefully, scientists found that their hair has no color, and each hair is hollow. The animals appear white because of light reflections inside each hair. In addition to each hair serving as an insulator, scientists believe that a polar bear's hair somehow changes light into heat, which is then carried to the bear's skin. Perhaps the hairs of polar bears are specialized solar cells. The air spaces in each hair prevent heat loss, and the fur itself is a blanket. The hairs seem to generate heat as well as hold it. Perhaps in the future our winter clothes will somehow use the idea behind the bear's special solar cells.

Regardless of the kind of clothing we wear in winter—down, wool, synthetics, or polar-bear hairs—we should wear several layers; and the clothing should fit loosely. Remember that an Eskimo's clothing is so loose a person can turn around inside it.

Hypothermia

If you ski or backpack in cold weather you've probably heard about hypothermia. If you haven't, it's something you should know about. The word comes from "hypo" which means under, and "therm" which means heat. So hypothermia means underheating, cooling, or even freezing, of the body. The cooling could be fast enough to kill a person. Outside air temperature doesn't have to be very low. In fact, hypothermia can happen when the temperature is 40° or 50°, and it often does.

Hypothermia is the chilling of the inner core of the body, as well as the brain. When that happens there is rapid physical and mental collapse. People's memory lags, they may have trouble saying words properly, and they may fall down or drop things because their muscles aren't working properly. You remember the story of Jean Hilliard and how she collapsed before she could rap on her neighbor's door.

For the body to operate properly, its temperature must remain around 98.6°. People produce more heat than they need, so they usually must get rid of the excess. In hypothermia the body loses more heat than it produces. This condition often occurs when a person gets wet. That's because most insulation does not work well when it is wet. The water pushes out the dead air, and water is not a good insulator. One of the deadliest accidents that can happen to a fisherman is to be washed overboard. Fishermen describe a 50-50-50 Law of Survival: When the water is 50° a person has only a 50% chance of surviving for 50 minutes.

```
┌─────────────────────────────────────────┐
│   SYMPTOMS of HYPOTHERMIA                │
│  WHEN EXPOSED TO WIND, COLD OR WET WATCH FOR: │
│  1. shivering                           │
│  2. vague, slow, slurred speech         │
│  3. memory lapses, incoherence, abnormal behavior │
│  4. immobile, fumbling hands.           │
│  5. undue stumbling... lurching gait    │
│  6. drowsiness (to sleep is to die)     │
│  7. exhaustion... too tired to get up after a rest │
│  8. unnoticed loss of clothing such as hat or glove │
└─────────────────────────────────────────┘
```

Wind also speeds up heat loss; it speeds evaporation. Wet clothing exposed to the wind is dangerous. The wind cools the water. When water reaches 50° it is unbearably cold. If it is held against a person by sopping clothing, heat moves rapidly from the body to the water.

Whenever you're outside, keep dry. Wear rain clothes. Also, wear wool. It's the one fiber that remains an insulator, though not a good one, even when it is wet.

While you're moving, hiking or skiing for example, your body makes a lot more heat than it does when it is at rest. That's why some hikers don't realize they can suffer from hypothermia. They think they can go on and on, even though they may be wet and cold. But that is when they should be most careful. If they are in the woods, they should get out of the wind, make camp, and build a fire.

If they don't, they may find that once they stop hiking, their production of body heat may drop suddenly by as much as 50%. They may start to shiver and become unable to control the shivering. They may slip into hypothermia; their speech will slow, they won't remember well, they will stumble and find they cannot hold things. They may become exhausted and drowsy, but they must not sleep—that would mean their end.

Those suffering from hypothermia will find it difficult if not impossible to help themselves. However, there are ways that other people can help.

HOW TO HELP A HYPOTHERMIA VICTIM

1. Take the victim to a protected place out of the wind and rain.

2. Remove the victim's clothing immediately. (That may mean stripping completely.)

3. If the person is able to drink, warm fluids should be given.

4. Dress the victim in warm, dry clothes or put into a warm sleeping bag.
KEEP THE VICTIM AWAKE.

In more advanced hypothermia, a person may be only semiconscious. It's important that the victim be kept awake and somehow be given warm fluids. Once stripped, the patient should be sandwiched in a large sleeping bag between two other people who are also stripped. They become heat donors to the person suffering hypothermia.

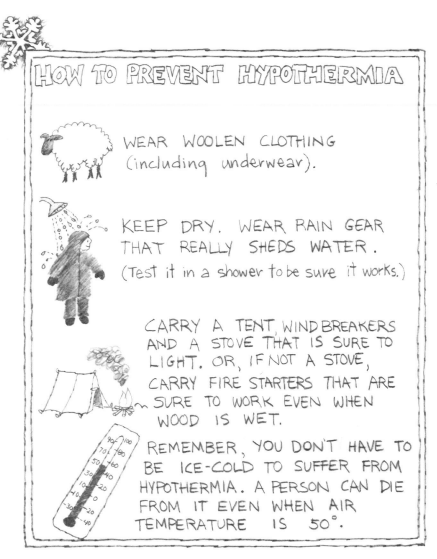

HOW TO PREVENT HYPOTHERMIA

WEAR WOOLEN CLOTHING (including underwear).

KEEP DRY. WEAR RAIN GEAR THAT REALLY SHEDS WATER. (Test it in a shower to be sure it works.)

CARRY A TENT, WIND BREAKERS AND A STOVE THAT IS SURE TO LIGHT. OR, IF NOT A STOVE, CARRY FIRE STARTERS THAT ARE SURE TO WORK EVEN WHEN WOOD IS WET.

REMEMBER, YOU DON'T HAVE TO BE ICE-COLD TO SUFFER FROM HYPOTHERMIA. A PERSON CAN DIE FROM IT EVEN WHEN AIR TEMPERATURE IS 50°.

Hopefully you'll never suffer from hypothermia. If you ski or backpack, take precautions because it can happen to you. Keep warm when outside, keep active but do not become exhausted, know when to quit, and keep dry. There are many things you can do to keep toasty warm, even when the temperature hovers around zero.

Astronauts use many of the ideas you have learned about keeping warm and keeping cool. The problems are severe in outer space because it gets both very cold and very hot there.

8/Keeping Warm in

Outer Space

Space is unbearably cold; the temperature is only a few degrees above minus 459.7°. That's absolute zero, the coldest anything can get. It is the absence of all heat.

At the same time, space is unbearably hot. That is, unless you are in the farthest parts of the solar system, far from the sun, or from any other star.

In Earth's atmosphere, the air serves as an insulating blanket. In daytime the air blanket filters sunlight, and so the Earth's surface does not receive its full strength. At night the air keeps the surface from losing heat rapidly. The night half of Earth cools somewhat because heat radiates from the planet. But the atmosphere is a barrier to radiation; it slows down the rate, and so there is only a moderate amount of cooling.

Temperature variations in space are far more extreme than those here on this planet. There is no atmosphere in space, so sunlight shines with full force. It is unfiltered. If you were exposed to it, you would feel hot immediately. On the moon, which also has no atmosphere, the temperature of the parts exposed to sunlight soars to 250° or thereabouts. But if you took a step or two and got behind a large boulder, the temperature in the shadow would be about 250° below zero. Not only does Earth's atmosphere filter sunlight, it also serves to distribute heat. Here on Earth a beach umbrella protects you from the sun, but it is still warm under the umbrella. On the moon, it would be different. The temperature under the umbrella would be hundreds of degrees colder than the surrounding region.

Moon rocks get very hot in sunlight. But as soon as the moon turns so those hot rocks are no longer receiving sunlight, the temperature of the rocks plummets. It's because radiation is so rapid. There's nothing to stop the radiation. The difference between the temperature of the rocks and space is so large that radiation occurs almost instantaneously. After only a few moments, those hot rocks are ice-cold.

Temperature control is a major problem that engineers face when they design space satellites and vehicles, such as the shuttle orbiters. The part of a ship receiving sunlight becomes very hot. At the same time, the part away from the sun is ice-cold. Ships must be well insulated to hold internal heat, and to keep out external heat. Temperature is evened out somewhat by turning the ship alternately toward the sun to pick up heat and away from it to cool hot surfaces by radiation.

Inside the orbiter, crew members are in a "shirt sleeve" environment—no special kind of clothing is needed. The temperature is kept at a comfortable level, and the air is recycled so it is always breathable. Outside the ship, or on the moon, an astronaut must wear a space suit. Without it, a person would swell up like a balloon because there would be no pressure on body liquids. They would change to gases and expand explosively. The half of a person facing the sun would get hot immediately, and the half away from it would be freezing cold. Just as the orbiter must be well insulated, so also must a space suit. Actually, a space suit is a miniature spaceship as far as temperature and other environment controls are concerned.

A space suit is an extremely complicated piece of equipment. (That's why each one costs about two million dollars.) It is white to reflect sunlight. Even so, the outer surface gets hot, so the suit is made in layers with air spaces between them. Three of the surfaces are shiny to reflect radiant heat.

The insulation of the suit prevents extreme changes caused by high and low external temperatures. But at the same time, the extreme insulation prevents the release of heat from the astronaut's body. As you learned earlier, your body produces more heat than you require, so there must be ways for that heat to escape. While insulation keeps an astronaut from overheating by the sun, heat from the astronaut's body could become a problem.

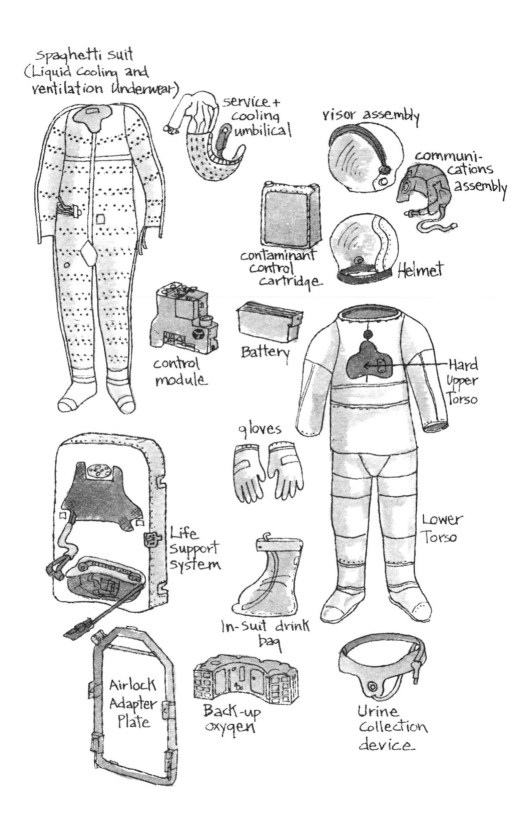

spaghetti suit
(Liquid Cooling and
ventilation Underwear)

service +
cooling
umbilical

visor assembly

communi-
cations
assembly

contaminant
control
cartridge

Helmet

control
module

Battery

Hard
Upper
Torso

gloves

Lower
Torso

Life
Support
system

In-suit drink
bag

Airlock
Adapter
Plate

Back-up
oxygen

Urine
Collection
device

Here on Earth each person produces about as much heat as a 100-watt light bulb. As you become active you really "light up"—you may produce more energy than half a dozen light bulbs. If you were in outer space, the same amount of heat would be generated. On Earth, the heat is carried away by both the evaporation of perspiration and the air that moves around you. So the same conditions must be set up inside a space suit; perspiration must evaporate and heat must be removed.

This is done by a liquid cooling system. Under the outer suit, astronauts wear what looks like a suit of long underwear. A system of 300 feet of narrow plastic tubes is built into the suit—it is called the "spaghetti suit." A small electric pump pushes water through the tubes, and the water picks up body heat. (A small amount of water can hold a large amount of heat.) The tubes carry the water to an evaporator outside the suit. There water is sprayed on the tubes. This water evaporates rapidly, and so cools the water inside the tubes. That water continues to circulate through the spaghetti suit, picking up heat and dumping it into space. About a quart of cooling water is used up and vented into space every hour. A tube leading to the mouth enables the astronaut to tap a reserve supply of drinking water. The water supply becomes one of the factors that limits the amount of time an astronaut can spend inside the suit.

There are others. For example, oxygen must be supplied to the astronaut and carbon dioxide and moisture from the body and from exhaled breath must be removed. The carbon dioxide is picked up by a filtering device, and the moisture is removed by a dehumidifier. Eventually both of these devices become saturated. Another limiting factor is the accumulation of urine and solid body wastes. Each suit is equipped with a one-quart urine holding bag. Also, astronauts wear diapers just in case they happen to be "caught short." So far astronauts have not been bedeviled by such problems. Nevertheless, one must be prepared should they occur.

High-Level Radiation

A hazard peculiar to outer space is what is called high-level radiation. In addition to the heat and light that Earth dwellers are aware of, the sun also produces other types of energy such as radio waves, ultraviolet rays, X rays, and gamma rays. Some of the ultraviolet radiation reaches us; it's what causes sunburn. But most is filtered out by the atmosphere, along with the X rays and gamma rays. In outer space an astronaut is bombarded by the full intensity of these rays, and it can be lethal. Suits must be designed so this high-energy radiation does not reach the astronaut. Even so, an astronaut cannot be fully protected—some of the radiation must be picked up. Fortunately, so far no serious aftereffects have been reported. However, longer exposure to this radiation is likely to be dangerous. This would especially be true should astronauts be working farther out in space than today's shuttle orbiters go.

Another hazard of space is the solar wind. While the sun gives off radiation such as that mentioned above, it also releases subatomic particles—pieces of atoms. These are thrown into space from the solar surface, and they stream throughout the solar system. The particles are electrified and so are attracted by magnetic fields. Earth's field pulls them in, and the particles form into "stretched-out-doughnut-shaped" clouds. They are clouds of high-energy particles that surround the planet. Long exposure to them would be harmful to astronauts. Therefore, space vehicles move through them rapidly. Those vehicles that remain in orbit are located outside the rings of solar particles or in regions where they are not so densely packed together.

Still other hazards that must be guarded against are micrometeoroids. Space is far from empty. In fact, it abounds with small particles of matter that move at high speeds through the regions bounding the planets. A good many satellites have been bombarded by them, though it is thought none of the collisions has been great enough to knock out their instruments. Still, it is possible that a sizable meteoroid could collide with an astronaut. Therefore, space suits and visors must be rugged enough to withstand such impact. No suit could withstand a collision with a large meteoroid. There would be little hope for an astronaut who was struck by one. Although there are billions of micrometeoroids (it is estimated that some 20,000 tons fall on Earth every day), fortunately larger ones are extremely rare.

Considering all the hazards that space suits must surmount, they are remarkably comfortable. Astronauts are severely restricted, of course. Their movements are rather awkward, but space suits of the 80s are well on the way to permitting missions of several hours' duration, and to permitting astronauts freedom of movement. They need this freedom to perform the many tasks that are planned for the next several years of space exploration.

Space suits are no longer custom-made. Originally each

astronaut had a particular suit that was especially made to fit that astronaut. Now there are three standard sizes—small, medium, and large—which is enough range to fit small and large astronauts, women as well as men.

The suits are made in three main pieces—the lower torso, upper torso, and helmet. The astronaut first dons a spaghetti suit and then puts on the lower section. Boots are attached to it. The torso is more solid fiberglass. A person puts it on by moving upward into it; the astronaut squats below it to enter. The lower garment and the arms of the torso are supple enough to bend easily at the joints.

SPAGHETTI SUIT   LOWER TORSO

The two sections are joined by a waist belt. Gloves are put on and then the helmet is locked into place. The astronaut is inside a "private spaceship." Before the astronaut leaves the orbiter, pure oxygen is breathed to remove nitrogen from the body. If this were not done, the astronaut would get the "bends," a bubbling of gases in the blood which is severely painful and can be fatal. The final operation is to put the visor assembly over the helmet. The astronaut adjusts the visor to provide maximum protection from brilliant sunshine.

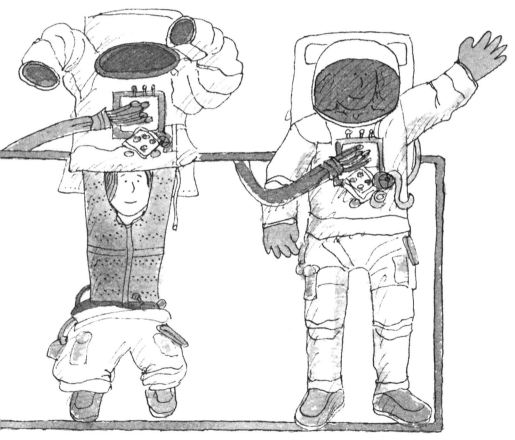

UPPER TORSO

BELT, HELMET,
VISOR, GLOVES

In the next few years space suited astronauts will be spending considerable time outside their mother ship. They will repair and make adjustments to space telescopes, and catch and repair satellites now in orbit that may either become damaged by meteorites or simply need an adjustment. Eventually it's expected that astronauts will be building space stations—permanent space platforms. They may also build solar power satellites, devices designed to trap solar energy, convert the energy to electricity, and relay the electricity by microwaves to Earth stations. The possibilities are endless. Perhaps astronauts will be building space factories or even entire colonies.

Possibly you will become one of these astronauts, for a good many will be needed during the closing decades of the 20th century. But whether you're up there in outer space, or here on Earth skiing down a slope, or winter backpacking through a wilderness, keep warm. Your body does a fine job of regulating your temperature, keeping you at a steady 98.6°, but now and then it can use a bit of assistance.

Further
Reading

Index

Further Reading

Branley, Franklyn M. *Energy for the 21st Century*. New York: Thomas Y. Crowell, 1975.

———. *Feast or Famine? The Energy Future*. New York: Thomas Y. Crowell, 1980.

Kelley, James B. "Heat, Cold and Clothing." *Scientific American*, February 1956: pp. 109–16.

"The Science—and Art—of Keeping Warm." *Natural History*, Vol. 90, No. 10 (1981): pp. 24–125.

Webbon, Bruce. "Survival in Space." *Natural History*, December 1981: pp. 50–57.

Index

Page numbers in *italics* refer to illustrations

active solar houses, 64, *64*

air

 dehumidifying of, 59–60, 81

 dry, 25–26, 59–60

 filtering of, 59

 humidifying of, 59–60

 movement of, 16, 19–21, *19*, *20*, 54–56, *55*, 58–60, *59*, 64, 66

air conditioning, 60

air ducts, 55, *55*, 56, 58, 60, *60*

alcohol, 16

animals, 11–13, 47. *See also* specific animals.

animal skins, 12, 29–30, *29*, *30*, *31*, 32, 35–37, *36*, *37*, 39, 51

Antarctica, 27

Army, U.S., 27

astronauts, 75, 77, 79–86, *84*, *85*, *86*

atoms, 82–83

basal metabolism, 27

"bends," 85

birds, 11–12, *11*, *12*, 30, 41, *41*, *42*, 43–47, *43*, *44*, *47*, 49

 body heat of, 43–47, *44*

 feathers of, as insulation, 46–47

[91]

birds, *continued*
    food and, *43*, 44–45, 46–47, *47*
    shivering and, 44–45, *47*
    surface vs. volume of, 43–44
black bears, 47–51, *48, 49, 51*
body heat, 7, 29, 39, 41, 43, 57
    blood supply and, 28
    production of, 10–11, 13, 44–47,
        49–51, 69, 71, 72, 79, 81
    See also heat conservation; tempera-
        ture, of human body.
body heat loss, 7, 35, 51, 57, 79, 81
    by breathing, 16, *16, 22*
    clothes and, 7, 25–26, 28, 36–41,
        57, 69–70
    by conduction, 21–23, *21, 22, 23*
    by convection, 20, *21*
    by evaporation, 15–16, *17, 17, 18,*
        22, 23, 25–26, 28, 37, 39, *72,*
        81
    goose bumps and, 11–13, *12*
    hypothermia and, 8–10, 13, 71–75
    shivering and, 10–11, 44–45, 47,
        72, *72*
    See also insulation; shelters.
brain, 69, 71
breathing, 16, *16, 22*, 81
breathing troubles, 59
bricks, 54, 56, 58, 64

caribou, 30, *30*, 36, *36*
carpets, 21, *21, 22*
Celsius, 7
central heating, 58–66
chemical industry, 66
chimney effect, 38
chimneys, 54–55, *55*, 56, 59
circulator pumps, 65, *65*
clothing, 7, *25*, 72
    in cold weather, 18, 26, 28, *28,*
        36–41, *36, 37, 38, 40, 41*, 57,
        68, 69–70, *69*, 72, *73, 74, 75*

clothing, *continued*
    of desert dwellers, *24*, 25–26, *26*
    evaporation and, 16
    radiation and, 18
    See also space suits.
coal, 58, 63–64
concrete, 64
conduction, 21–23, *21, 22, 23*, 36,
    56
convection, 19–22, *17, 19, 20, 22,*
    23, 31–32, 34, 36, 58, *59*, 60–
    61, *60, 61*

deer, 30, 36. *See also* caribou; rein-
    deer.
defecation, 50, 82
desert dwellers, *24*, 25–26, *25, 26*
doors, glass, 55, *55*
down, as insulation, 41, 57, 69–70

Earth, 77, 81
    atmosphere of, 77–78, 82–83, 86
    magnetic fields of, 82–83
Earth stations, 86
electricity, 65–67, 86
energy, production of, 10–11, 27, 43,
    64, 66–67, 86
engineers, 66, 78
Eskimos, 23, 26–28
    clothing of, 26, 28, 37, *37, 38*, 39,
        70
    igloos of, 32–36, *33, 35*, 39
    shelters of, 28, 30–32, *30, 31*, 36
evaporation, 15–16, *17, 17, 18, 22,*
    23, 25–26, 28, 37, 39, 72, 81

Fahrenheit, 7
fans, 58, *59*
fats, 10, 27, 28, 49, 50
feathers, 11–12, 46–47, 57
fever, 16

50-50-50 Law of Survival, 71
fire, 52, 54–55, *54*, *55*, 56, 58, 59
fireplaces, 17, 53–56, *55*
  as air circulators, 56
  "cooking," 54–55, *54*, 56
  metal core of, 56
fish, 30
fishermen, 71
foil, 18
food, 10, 27, 28, 29, 30, 45, 46–47,
  47, 49–50, 51, *51*
forced hot-air heating, 58–61, *59*, *60*,
  63
fuel, 58, 62–64, 66
furnaces, 55, 60–61, *60*, *61*, 63
  hot-air registers of, 58, *59*
  single-register, 58
  wood-burning, 58–59, *59*, 63

gamma rays, 82
gas, as fuel, 63–64, 66
gases, of human body, 10, 79, 81,
  85
glass wool, 30, 62
goose bumps, 11–13, *12*
grass, dried, 29, 30, *30*, *31*, 49, 51,
  53
greenhouses, 64

hay fever, 59
heat, 7, 15, 17, 66, 82
heat, body. *See* body heat.
heat conservation, 11–13, 36
  reduction of body surface and, 27–
  28, 51, 57
  See also clothing; goose bumps; insulation; shelters.
heat loss, 7, *14*, 15–23, *17*, 27–28,
  44–47, 49–51, 53, 54–55, 57,
  61–62, 69–75, 81
  by breathing, 16, *16*, 22, 81

heat loss, *continued*
  by conduction, 21–23, *21*, *22*, *23*,
  36, 56
  by convection, *17*, 19–22, *19*, *20*,
  22, *23*, 31–32, 34, 36, 58, 59,
  60–61, *60*, *61*
  by evaporation, 15–16, *17*, *17*, *18*,
  22, *23*, 25–26, 28, 37, 39, 72,
  81
  prevention of, 11–13, 27–28, 49–
  51, 55–57. *See also* clothing;
  insulation; shelters.
  by radiation, 16–19, *17*, *22*, *23*, 36,
  46, 54–56, 60–61, *60*, *61*, 77–
  79
heat pumps, 66
heat-recycling houses, 65–66, *65*
hibernation, 49–51
Hilliard, Jean, 8–10, 13, 71
hot-water heating systems, 60–61, *60*.
  See also active solar houses; heat-
  recycling houses.
houses, 52, 53–60, 61–66, *62*, *64*, *65*,
  67
  in Colonial America, 53–55, 56, 61
  heat-recycling, 65–66, *65*
  humidity level in, 59–60
  in eighteenth-century America, 56–
  58
human skin, 9, 13, 15, 25, 26–28
hydrogen, 66
hydropower, 66
hypothermia, 8–10, 13, 71–75, *72*,
  73, *74*

ice water, 22, *23*
igloos, 32–36, *33*, *35*, 39
Indians, American, 31
insulation, 7, 61, 64
  animal skins and, 29–30, *30*, *31*,
  32, 35–37, *36*, *37*, 39

[93]

insulation, *continued*
clothing and, 7, 18, 26, 28, 36–41, *37, 38, 40, 41,* 46, 53, 69–70, *72, 73, 74*
dead air as, 12–13, 36, *36,* 41, 46, 51, 62, *62,* 69–70, 71, 79
dried grass and, 29–30, *30, 31,* 49, 51, 53
Earth's atmosphere as, 77–78, 82
feathers and, 11–12, 46, 57
goose bumps and, 11–13, *12*
hair and, 36–37, *36,* 51, 69, 70
snow and, 29–31
space suits and, 79
of space vehicles, 78–79

Laplanders, 23, 26–27, 29, *29*
leather, 36
logs, 29, 49

meat, 27, 28
metal, 22, 56
meteorites, 86
meteoroids, 83
microwaves, 86
milk, 50
moisture, 25–26, 59–60, 62, 81
moon, 76, 77–78, 79
moon rocks, 78
motors, electric, 58
muscles, 10–11, 13, 44

nitrogen, 85
nomads, 29
north-country people, 23, 26–39
nuclear fusion, 66–67

oil, as fuel, 62–63, 66
oil lamps, 32, 35, 39
outer space, 76, 77, 81, 82
exploration of, 83, 86
temperature variations in, 77–79
oxygen, 10, 55, 56, 81, 85

passive solar houses, 64, *64*
perspiration, 26, 39, 81
Pilgrims, 53
plastic, 66
plastic foam, as insulator, 62
polar bears, 70, *70,* 75
Polarguard, 70
pores, 15
protein, 27, 28

radiant heat, *15,* 16–19, *17, 18,* 22, 23, 36, 46, 54–56, 60–61, *60, 61,* 77–79
via electric wires, 18
foil and, 18
via hot-water pipes, 18
via radiators, 20, 60–61, *60, 61*
radiation, high level, 82
radiators, 20, 60–61, *60, 61*
radio waves, 82
refrigerators, 15, 66
reindeer, 29, 32
rock wool, as insulation, 62
rodents, 62, 63
rubber, 22

satellites, 78, 83, 86
solar power, 86
sealskins, 30, *31,* 35
shelters, 24, 28–36, *29, 30, 31, 33, 34, 35*
shivering, 10–11, *10,* 44–45, 47, 72, *72*
shuttle orbiters, 78, 82–83, 85
skin, animal. *See* animal skins.
skin, human. *See* human skin.
snow, 29, 30–31, 32–36, 39, 53, 57
solar cells, 70
solar collectors, 64
solar-electric generators, 66
solar energy, 64–66, 86

solar heat, 64–66, *65*
solar particles, 83
solar surface, 82
solar system, 77, 82–83, 86
solar wind, 82–83
space stations, 86
space suits, 79, 80, 81–86, *84, 85, 86*
    liquid cooling system of ("spaghetti suit"), *80, 81, 84, 84*
space telescopes, 86
space vehicles, 78, 79, 82–83, 85, 86
stars, 76, 77
steam heat, 61, *61*, 63
stones, 54, 56, 64
storm sashes, 62, *62*
stoves, 17, 54, 56–58, *57*, 74
subatomic particles, 82–83
sun, 77, 79, 82–83
sunburn, 82
sunlight, 26, 77–79, 82, 85
synthetic fabrics, 66, 70

teepees, 31
telescopes. *See* space telescopes.
temperature
    of human body, 7–8, 9, 10–13, 15, 16, 25–28, 45, 69, 71–75, 86
    of outer space, 77–79
    of space suits, 79

temperature, *continued*
    of space vehicles, 79
    See also insulation.
thermal blankets, 18
Thermolactyl, 70
thermostat, 55
30-30-30 Rule for Survival, 27
tile, 21–22, *21, 22*
trees, 49

ultraviolet rays, 82
urination, 50, *80*, 82

warming pans, 58, *58*
water, 15, 19–20
    evaporation of, 15–16, 17, *17*, 18, *22, 23*, 25–26, 28, 37, 39, 72, 81
    hypothermia and, 71–72, *72, 73, 74*
whale bones, 30, 32
whales, 30
wind, 26–27, *72, 73*
    solar, 82–83
wood, 29
    burning of, for heat, 10, 54, 58–59, *59*, 63–64, 74
    as conductor of heat, 21–22
    green, 53, 61

X rays, 82